Stoke City
Quiz Book

101 Multiple Choice Questions To Test Your Knowledge Of This Wonderful Football Club

Published by Glowworm Press
7 Nuffield Way
Abingdon OX14 1RL

By Chris Carpenter

Stoke City Football Club

This book contains one hundred and one informative and entertaining trivia questions with multiple choice answers. With 101 questions, some easy, some more challenging, this entertaining book will really test your knowledge of the club.

You will be quizzed on a wide range of topics associated with **Stoke City Football Club** for you to test yourself, with questions on players, legends, managers, opponents, transfer deals, trophies, records, fixtures, songs and more, guaranteeing you both an educational experience and hours of fun. The Stoke City Quiz Book will provide the ultimate in entertainment for fans of all ages, and will certainly test your knowledge. The book is packed with information and is a must-have for all loyal Stoke fans.

2019/20 Season Edition

FOREWORD

When I was asked to write a foreword to
this book I was flattered.

I have known the author Chris Carpenter
for many years and his knowledge of facts
and figures is phenomenal.

His love for football and his skill in writing
quiz books make him the ideal man to pay
homage to my great love Stoke City
Football Club.

This book came about as a result of a
challenge in a Lebanese restaurant of all
places!

I do hope you enjoy the book.

Lloyd Hudson
Season Ticket Holder of many years

Let's start with some relatively easy questions.

1. When were Stoke City founded?
    A. 1863
    B. 1868
    C. 1873

2. What is Stoke City's nickname?
    A. The Potters
    B. The Ramblers
    C. The Strollers

3. Where do Stoke City play their home games?
    A. The Bet365 Stadium
    B. The Britannia Stadium
    C. The Nationwide Stadium

4. What is the stadium's capacity?
    A. 30,089
    B. 30,890
    C. 30,908

5. Who or what is the club mascot?
    A. Pottermus Hippo
    B. Pottersauraus Rex
    C. Potterabout Rhino

6. Who has made the most appearances for the club in total?
    A. Jackie Marsh
    B. John McCue

C. Denis Smith

7. Who is the club's record goal scorer?
   A. Peter Crouch
   B. John Ritchie
   C. Eric Skeels

8. Who is the fastest ever goal scorer for the club?
   A. Asmir Begovic
   B. Kenwyne Jones
   C. Charlie Wilson

9. What song do the players run out to?
   A. City til I die
   B. We'll be with you
   C. Delilah

10. Which of these is a well known pub near the ground?
    A. Halfway House
    B. Harvester
    C. Queensway

OK, so here are the answers to the first ten questions. If you get seven or more right, you are off to a good start but be warned, the questions do get harder.

A1. Stoke City was founded as Stoke Ramblers in 1863, although the first records of them playing an actual game was in October 1868, so we will accept either answer. The club turned professional in August 1885, and in 1888 became founder members of the Football League. In 1925 the club changed its name to Stoke City.

A2. The club's nickname is 'The Potters', named after the pottery industry in Stoke-on-Trent.

A3. Stoke City play at the Bet365 Stadium. It was renamed from the Britannia Stadium in June 2016.

A4. Thanks to recent renovations, the current capacity of the Bet365 Stadium is now 30,089 spectators.

A5. Pottermus Hippo is Stoke City's mascot. Oddly, the cuddly blue hippo can be booked to attend weddings.

A6. Club legend John McCue made 675 appearances for the Potters, more than anyone else in total.

A7. John Ritchie is Stoke City's highest ever goal scorer, finding the back of the net a record 176 times in 347 appearances. Now, that's impressive.

A8. Surprisingly Asmir Begovic is the club's fastest ever goal scorer, scoring just 13 seconds after kick-off, a world record for a goalkeeper. He scored with a kick up-field from his own penalty box in a match against Southampton on 2nd November 2013.

A9. Stoke City players run out of the tunnel to the song 'We'll be with you'. The song, which dates back to 1972, was written by David Trent, who also wrote the words to the theme tune to the TV show Neighbours.

A10. The Harvester is a well known chain pub/restaurant right next to the stadium. Be prepared to queue for a pint though.

OK, here are some ground related questions.

11. Where did Stoke City play their home games before the current stadium location?
    A. Railway Ground
    B. Ventura Ground
    C. Victoria Ground

12. What is the club's record attendance?
    A. 50,750
    B. 51,380
    C. 52,736

13. When did the club move to the new stadium?
    A. 1995
    B. 1997
    C. 1999

14. Why is it called the Bet365 Stadium?
    A. Named after a betting company
    B. Named after a competition that was held daily in 2015
    C. Chosen by most votes in an online competition

15. What was there before the stadium was built?

A. Coal Mine
B. Garden Centre
C. Warehousing

16. What is the name of the road the stadium is on?
    A. Britannia Boulevard
    B. Stanley Matthews Way
    C. Stone Road

17. Which stand has the biggest capacity?
    A. Boothen End
    B. East Stand
    C. West Stand

18.   Where do the away fans sit in the ground?
    A. North Stand
    B. South Stand
    C. West Stand

19. What is the size of the pitch?
    A. 109 x 70 yards
    B. 110 x 73 yards
    C. 118 x 72 yards

20.   Which of these artists has played a concert at the ground?
    A. Bryan Adams
    B. Elton John
    C. Bon Jovi

Here are the answers to the last set of questions.

A11. Stoke used to play home games at the atmospheric Victoria Ground.

A12. The club's record attendance is 51,380 against Arsenal on the 29th March 1937 at the Victoria Ground.

A13. After 119 years at the Victoria Ground, the longest time spent at a ground by any team in Britain, Stoke moved to the brand new purpose built Britannia Stadium in August 1997, ready for the start of the 1997/98 season. The stadium cost £15 million to build, which seemed a lot of money at the time.

A14. Bet365 is an online betting company.

A15. The ground was built on the site of the former Stafford Number 2 Colliery.

A16. The Bet365 Stadium is located on Stanley Matthews Way.

A17. The East Stand can hold 8,789 spectators, the most of the four stands, with everyone seated.

A18. The South Stand is used by both home and away supporters.

A19. The official size of Stoke City's pitch is 109 yards long and 70 yards wide. As a comparison, Wembley Stadium's pitch is 115 yards long and 75 yards wide.

A20. All three have performed at the stadium. Give yourself a bonus point if you knew that.

Here is the next set of ten questions.

21. What is the club's record win in any competition?
    A. 20-0
    B. 22-0
    C. 26-0

22. Who did they beat?
    A. Bad Cop
    B. Mow Cop
    C. Sheep Cop

23. What is the club's record win in the League?
    A. 8-3
    B. 9-3
    C. 10-3

24. Who did they beat?
    A. West Bromwich Albion
    B. West Ham United
    C. Wolverhampton Wanderers

25. What is the club's record win in the Premier League?
    A. 4-1
    B. 5-1
    C. 6-1

26. Who did they beat?
    A. Aston Villa
    B. Hull City

C. Liverpool

27.　　What is the club's record
defeat?
　　　A. 6–2
　　　B. 9–0
　　　C. 10-0

28.　　Who against?
　　　A. Liverpool
　　　B. Chelsea
　　　C. Preston North End

29.　　In which season?
　　　A. 1889/90
　　　B. 1909/10
　　　C. 1919/20

30.　　Who has scored the most hat
tricks for Stoke City?
　　　A. Alex Ormston
　　　B. Johnny King
　　　C. Sid Peppitt

Here are the answers to the last set of questions.

A21. The club's record win in any competition is 26–0.

A22. Stoke City beat village side Mow Cop 26–0 in the Staffordshire Senior Cup, in 1877 against Mow Cop. Yes, it was an officially recognised match, and so that is what is shown in the record books.

A23. Stoke City's record league win is 10-3.

A24. Stoke City trounced West Bromwich Albion in the First Division on the 4th February 1937.

A25. Stoke City's record Premier League win is 6-1.

A26. Stoke City thrashed Liverpool 6-1 on the 24th May 2015.

A27. The club's record defeat is 0-10.

A28. The match was against Preston North End.

A29. The club's heaviest ever defeat occurred on the 14th September 1889, so it was in the 1889/90 season.

A30. Johnny King scored 5 hat tricks in total for the club, which is more than anyone else.

Here is the next set of questions.

31. When did the club win their first ever league title (the Football Alliance)?
    A. 1891/92
    B. 1911/12
    C. 1921/22

32. How many times have Stoke City won the League?
    A. 0
    B. 1
    C. 2

33. How many times have Stoke City won the FA Cup?
    A. 0
    B. 1
    C. 2

34. How many times have they won the League Cup?
    A. 0
    B. 1
    C. 2

35. What is the furthest stage the club has reached in the FA Cup?
    A. Quarter Final
    B. Semi Final
    C. Final

36.　　Who did they lose to?
   A. Manchester City
   B. Manchester United
   C. Leeds United

37.　　When did the club win the
   League Cup?
   A. 1970
   B. 1971
   C. 1972

38.　　Who did they beat in the final?
   A. Arsenal
   B. Chelsea
   C. Tottenham Hotspur

39.　　What was the score?
   A. 1-0
   B. 2-1
   C. 3-2

40.　　Who scored the winning goal
   in the League Cup final?
   A. Terry Conroy
   B. George Eastham
   C. Mark Stein

Here are the answers to the last block of questions.

A31. 1890/91 was a successful season with Stoke City winning the club's first league title, the Football Alliance, and gaining re-election to the Football League.

A32. Stoke City have never won the top division League title.

A33. Stoke City have never won the FA Cup.

A34. Stoke City have won the League Cup once.

A35. Stoke City reached the final of the FA Cup at the end of the 2010/11 season. Having been the losing semi-finalist on three previous occasions, this was the first time the club had reached the FA Cup Final.

A36. Stoke City were defeated 1-0 by Manchester City in what was a very close game.

A37. Stoke City won the League Cup on the 4th March 1972 with the final taking place at Wembley Stadium. Of the eleven players who started for Stoke, ten were

English, and one, Terry Conroy, was Irish. How the game has changed!

A38. Stoke City beat Chelsea, who were strong favourites on the day.

A39. Stoke City beat Chelsea 2-1.

A40. Terry Conroy put Stoke ahead, Peter Osgood equalised just before half time; with George Eastham scoring the winning goal for Stoke in the 73rd minute.

I hope you're having fun, and getting most of the answers right.

41. What is the record transfer fee paid?
    A. £12.3 million
    B. £15.3 million
    C. £18.3 million

42.   Who was the record transfer fee paid for?
    A. Peter Crouch
    B. Giannelli Imbula
    C. Xherdan Shaqiri

43.   What is the record transfer fee received?
    A. £16 million
    B. £18 million
    C. £20 million

44.   Who was the record transfer fee received for?
    A. Marko Arnautovic
    B. Asmir Begovic
    C. Steven N'Zonzi

45.   Who was the first Stoke City player to play for England?
    A. Peter Dobing
    B. Stanley Matthews
    C. Mike Pejic

46.   Who won the most international caps whilst a Stoke City player?
    A. William Maxwell
    B. Mike Sheron
    C. Glenn Whelan

47.   Who is Stoke's leading goal scorer in European football?
    A. Ben Barber
    B. Kenwyne Jones
    C. Joel Taylor

48.   Who is the youngest player ever to represent the club?
    A. Peter Bullock
    B. Lárus Sigurðsson
    C. Mart Watkins

49.   Who is the youngest ever goal scorer?
    A. Peter Bullock
    B. Roy Vernon
    C. Mart Watkins

50.   Who is the oldest player ever to represent the club?
    A. Tony Allen
    B. Keith Bebbington
    C. Stanley Matthews

Here are the answers to the last set of questions.

A41. Stoke City's record signing fee is £18.3 million.

A42. Defensive midfielder Giannelli Imbula arrived from Porto in January 2016 for £18.3 million. His transfer eclipsed the £12 million previous record signing of Shaqiri in August 2015.

A43. In July 2017 Stoke City received £20 million for a winger, with the fee set to rise to £25 million depending upon milestones set in the contract.

A44. The club's record sale was for Marko Arnautovic, who went to Wet Ham United. His transfer eclipsed the £8 million previous record sale of Begovic to Chelsea in July 2015.

A45. Stanley Matthews was the first Stoke City player to play for England. He won his first England cap starring and scoring in a 4-0 victory against Wales in Cardiff on the 29th September 1934.

A46. Glenn Whelan won the most international caps whilst a Stoke player, making a total of 58 appearances for the Republic of Ireland.

A47. Kenwyne Jones is the club's leading goal scorer in Europe having scored four goals in the UEFA Europa League.

A48. The youngest player to represent Stoke City was Peter Bullock aged just 16 years and 163 days when he made his debut against Swansea City on the 19th April 1958.

A49. Peter Bullock is also Stoke's youngest ever goal scorer, scoring on his debut against Swansea City in the 4-1 win.

A50. Stanley Matthews is the oldest player ever to represent the club; aged 46 years and 281 days when he appeared against Derby County in the First Division on the 7th May 1921 in the final game of the 1920/21 season.

I hope you're learning some new facts about the Potters.

51. Who is Stoke City's leading scorer in the Premier League?
    A. Charlie Adam
    B. Peter Crouch
    C. Jonathan Walters

52. Who is the club's longest serving manager of all time?
    A. Mick Mills
    B. Thomas Stanley
    C. Tony Waddington

53. Who is the club's longest serving post war manager?
    A. Alan Durban
    B. Tony Pulis
    C. Tony Waddington

54. What is the name of the Stoke City match day programme?
    A. Potters Magazine
    B. Stoke Matchday Programme
    C. Stoke City Official Matchday Programme

55. From which club did Stoke sign Sam Vokes?
    A. Blackburn Rovers
    B. Bolton Wanderers
    C. Burnley

56. Which of these is a Stoke City fanzine?
   A. The Beefcake
   B. The Mudcake
   C. The Oatcake

57. What motif is on the club crest?
   A. A pottery stand
   B. Stoke-on-Trent coat of arms
   C. Team's colours and nickname

58. What is the club's motto?
   A. "Confidemus"
   B. "Consilio et anamis"
   C. "Vis Unita Fortior"

59. Who are considered as Stoke City's main rivals?
   A. Portsmouth
   B. Port Vale
   C. Preston

60. What could be regarded as the club's most well known song?
   A. The green, green grass of home
   B. Please release me
   C. Delilah

Here is the latest set of answers.

A51. It's neck and neck (oops, sorry Peter) with Crouchy just ahead of Walters. Walters scored 43 goals in The Premier League for the club, while Crouch scored 45.

A52. The longest serving manager in the club's history is Tony Waddington who was in charge of 764 matches in his reign from June 1960 to March 1977.

A53. The longest serving post war manager is also Tony Waddington.

A54. The name of the award winning matchday programme is Potters Magazine.

A55. Vokes signed from Burnley in January 2019, for an undisclosed fee.

A56. The Oatcake was the best known and most influential of the fanzines dedicated to Stoke City. It now has a popular online website.

A57. The club's badge is simply the team's colours and nickname.

A58. The club's Latin motto is "Vis Unita Fortior", and the English translation is "United Strength is Stronger".

A59. Port Vale are considered as Stoke's main rivals.

A60. Delilah has been the club anthem since the 1970s. The story goes that it was adopted by the fans after a supporter was heard singing it in a local pub. Altogether now... "I saw the light on the night that I passed by her window..."

Let's have some easy questions.

61. What is the traditional colour of the home shirt?
    A. Red and Black stripes
    B. Red and White stripes
    C. White and Black stripes

62. Who is the club captain for the 2019/20 season?
    A. Joe Allen
    B. James McClean
    C. Ryan Shawcross

63. Who is the current club sponsor?
    A. Betfair
    B. Bet365
    C. Bet666

64. Who was the first club sponsor?
    A. Carling
    B. Fradley Homes
    C. Ricoh

65. Who currently supplies kit to the first team?
    A. Adidas
    B. Macron
    C. Warrior

66. Which of these sports brands has not supplied kit to Stoke City?
   A. Nike
   B. Puma
   C. Umbro

67. Who is currently the club chairman?
   A. Gordon Banks
   B. Peter Coates
   C. Tony Scholes

68. Who started the 2019/20 season as manager?
   A. Mark Hughes
   B. Nathan Jones
   C. Gary Rowett

69. Who was the club's first ever match in the league against?
   A. West Bromwich Albion
   B. West Ham United
   C. Wolverhampton Wanderers

70. Who was the supporters' player of the year for 2019?
   A. Joe Allen
   B. Jack Butland
   C. Tom Edwards

Here are the answers to the last set of questions.

A61. Their traditional home kit is a red and white vertically striped shirt, normally combined with white shorts.

A62. Ryan Shawcross is the club captain for the 2019/20 season.

A63. The current club sponsor is gambling company Bet365.

A64. Japanese multinational imaging and electronics company Ricoh was the club's first sponsor with the name first appearing on the shirt in 1981.

A65. From the beginning of the 2016/17 season, the kit has been supplied by Macron.

A66. Nike has never supplied kit to Stoke, whereas Puma and Umbro, amongst others, have.

A67. Peter Coates is the current club chairman. Tony Scholes is the Chief Executive and Gordon Banks is of course the President.

A68. Nathan Jones started the 2019/20 season as manager. He was appointed to the role in January 2019.

A69. The first ever Stoke City league match was played against West Bromwich Albion on 8th September 1888 in the inaugural 1888/89 season.

A70. Jack Butland was voted as the player of the year for the 2019. Joe Allen was the player of the year for 2018.

Here is the next batch of ten carefully chosen questions.

71. Who scored the first goal at the current stadium?
    A. Dean Crowe
    B. Graham Kavanagh
    C. Ray Wallace

72. Which Stoke City legend's ashes were buried beneath the stadium's centre circle after he died in February 2000?
    A. Johnny King
    B. Sir Stanley Matthews
    C. Eric Skeels

73. Which player has made the most substitute appearances for Stoke City?
    A. Tony Allen
    B. Keith Bebbington
    C. Ricardo Fuller

74. Who scored Stoke's first ever goal?
    A. Henry Almond
    B. Alan Dodd
    C. Peter Fox

75. Who was the first manager in Stoke's history to reach the FA Cup Final?

A. George Eastham
B. Tony Pulis
C. Tony Waddington

76.   Which team did Stoke City
   beat in their biggest post war FA
   Cup Semi-Final victory?
      A. Bolton Wanderers
      B. Reading
      C. Sunderland

77. Which is Stoke City's best ever
   finish in the Premier League?
      A. 7th
      B. 9th
      C. 11th

78.   Which Stoke City goal keeper
   entered the Guinness World
   Records for the furthest goal scored
   in football?
      A. Asmir Begovic
      B. Bob Dixon
      C. John Farmer

79.   In which season did Stoke City
   have the most goalless draws?
      A. 1955/56
      B. 1978/79
      C. 2012/13

80.   What nationality is Bruno
   Martins Indi?

A. Belgian
B. Dutch
C. Portuguese

Here are the answers to the last block of questions.

A71. Graham Kavanagh had the honour of scoring the first goal at the new stadium, in a League cup game in August 1997 against Rochdale. He also scored the final ever goal at the Victoria Ground in a 2-1 over West Brom. Give yourself a bonus point if you knew that.

A72. After Sir Stanley Matthews died in February 2000, his ashes were buried beneath the stadium's centre circle.

A73. Ricardo Fuller has made the most substitute appearances with 71 for the club.

A74. Henry Almond, the club's founder, scored the club's first ever goal.

A75. Tony Pulis became the first manager in Stoke's history to reach an FA Cup Final.

A76. The famous win of 5-0 against Bolton Wanderers in April 2011 was the club's only FA Cup semi-final victory, which meant the club reached the FA Cup final for the first time ever. What a day.

A77. A ninth place finish in 2013/14 is Stoke City's best ever finish in the Premier League.

A78. Asmir Begovic scored from 97.5 yards in the 1-1 draw with Southampton on 2nd November 2013. His kick, after just 13 seconds, caught the wind and bounced over opposite number Artur Boruc into the Saints' net.

A79. The 2012/13 season featured Stoke having five goalless draws in the league.

A80. Bruno was born in Portugal, and moved, with his family, to The Netherlands aged just three months. He has won over 30 caps for the Netherlands national team.

Here are the next set of questions, let's hope you get most of them right.

81. Which player is credited with inventing the banana kick?
   A. Alan Durban
   B. Alan Hudson
   C. Johnny King

82. Which goalkeeper holds the record for most consecutive clean sheets at the club?
   A. Gordon Banks
   B. Peter Shilton
   C. Steve Simonsen

83. What shirt number does Tom Ince wear?
   A. 7
   B. 17
   C. 27

84. Which of these players is not part of Stoke's greatest ever XI?
   A. Ricardo Fuller
   B. Ryan Shawcross
   C. Peter Shilton

85. Who holds the record for most goals scored for Stoke City in a single match?
   A. Tony Allen
   B. Neville Coleman

C. Peter Fox

86.   Where is Stoke City's training ground?
   A. Clayton Wood Training Ground
   B. Stoke City Training Ground
   C. Victoria Training Ground

87.   Who was Stoke City's first full-time manager?
   A. Horace Austerberry
   B. Alfred Barker
   C. Thomas Slaney

88.   What is Stoke City's longest winning streak in the league?
   A. 6
   B. 8
   C. 10

89.   Who has scored the most penalties for the club?
   A. Ricardo Fuller
   B. Paul Maguire
   C. Jimmy McAlinden

90.   Who has made the most league appearances for the club?
   A. Tony Allen
   B. Bob McGrory
   C. Eric Skeels

Here are the answers to the last set of questions.

A81. Johnny King was one of the great footballers of the fifties and sixties, and he was credited with inventing the now infamous free kick technique - the 'banana kick'.

A82. During the 2006/07 season, Simonsen became the record holder for most consecutive clean sheets at Stoke City with seven.

A83. Tom Ince wears shirt number 7.

A84. Perhaps surprisingly it is the great Peter Shilton that was not included in the clubs greatest XI, as he lost out to England's greatest keeper of all time Gordon Banks.

A85. Neville Coleman netted seven in an 8-0 win over Lincoln City on the 23rd February 1957, and to this day holds the record for most goals scored by a single player in a game. It's not something that will be broken any time soon.

A86. Stoke's players put in the hours at Clayton Wood Training Ground.

A87. Thomas Slaney was the club's first full-time manager; and he was in charge for nine years from 1874 to 1883.

A88. Stoke City's longest sequence of League wins is 8 games spanning the 30th March 1895 until the 21st September 1895.

A89. The player who has scored the most penalties for the club is Paul Maguire who scored a total of ten successful spot kicks.

A90. Eric Skeels holds the record with 507 league appearances for the club from 1959 to 1976.

Here is the final set of questions. Enjoy!

91. In which year did Stoke City get promotion to the Premier League after a 23 year absence from the top flight?
   A. 1998
   B. 2003
   C. 2008

92. Which Stoke City midfielder was known for his long throws?
   A. Rory Delap
   B. Stephen Ireland
   C. Steve Sidwell

93. What number shirt did the legendary Stanley Matthews wear?
   A. 7
   B. 9
   C. 10

94. Which of these goal keepers achieved the longest run of clean sheets for Stoke City?
   A. Bob Dixon
   B. Steve Simonsen
   C. John Farmer

95. What shirt number does the mascot wear?
   A. 70
   B. 71

C. 72

96.   Which player was the first signing made by Mark Hughes?
    A. Dionatan Teixeira
    B. Phil Bardsley
    C. Erik Pieters

97.   What is the club's official club website?
    A. potters.co.uk
    B. scfcdirect.com
    C. stokecityfc.com

98.   Who was Stoke City's first overseas manager?
    A. Johan Boskamp
    B. Alan Durban
    C. Gudjon Thordarson

99.   Who is Stoke City's youngest player to score a hat-trick?
    A. Ricardo Fuller
    B. Paul Maguire
    C. Adam Rooney

100.   What is the club's official twitter account?
    A. @SCFC
    B. @StokeCity
    C. @StokeCityFC

101. Which Stoke City legend has a statue showing different stages of his career put up in his honour outside the ground?
A. Gordon Banks
B. Sir Stanley Matthews
C. John Ritchie

Here is the final last set of answers.

A91. On 4th May 2008, Stoke City won promotion to the top flight of English football after a 23 year absence, and 2008/09 became their first season in the Premier League.

A92. Rory Delap a midfielder by trade, was renowned for his long throw-in ability in his time in Stoke City

A93. Club legend Stanley Matthews wore the number 7 shirt.

A94. Steve Simonsen is the goalkeeper who has had the longest run of clean sheets in Stoke City.

A95. Pottermus Hippo, the mascot, wears shirt number 72, in homage to the club's League Cup win in 1972.

A96. The first signing under Mark Hughes was on 28th June 2013 with Dutch international left-back Erik Pieters arriving from PSV Eindhoven for a fee of £3 million.

A97. StokeCityFC.com is the official website address.

A98. Icelandic manager Gudjon Thordarson was Stoke City's first manager from overseas, taking over in November 1999. He was in charge for 154 games in total with a respectable win percentage of exactly 50%.

A99. In only his second full start for the club, aged just 18 years and 9 days Adam Rooney scored a hat trick in the 5-1 victory over Brighton & Hove Albion on the 30th April 2006. Last we heard, he is still playing professional football, and still scoring goals, up in Scotland.

A100. @StokeCity is the club's official twitter account. It tweets multiple times daily and has over a million followers.

A101. There are three nine-foot statues of Sir Stanley Matthews outside the ground, showing Sir Stan at different stages of his thirty year career. The memorial was officially unveiled in October 2001.

That's it. That's a great question to finish with. I hope you enjoyed this book, and I hope you got most of the answers right.

I also hope you learnt some new facts about the club, and if you saw anything wrong, or have a general comment, please visit the glowwormpress.com website.

Thanks for reading, and if you did enjoy the book, would you be so kind as leave a positive review on Amazon.

Printed in Great Britain
by Amazon

32513591R00031